# Germany

## Tradition, Culture, and Daily Life

### MAJOR NATIONS IN A GLOBAL WORLD

# Books in the Series

Australia

Brazil

China

France

Germany

India

Italy

Japan

Mexico

Russia

South Africa

United Kingdom

# Germany

## Tradition, Culture, and Daily Life

**MAJOR NATIONS IN A GLOBAL WORLD**

John Perritano

Mason Crest

Mason Crest
450 Parkway Drive, Suite D
Broomall, PA 19008
www.masoncrest.com

Printed and bound in the United States of America.

First printing
9 8 7 6 5 4 3 2 1

Series ISBN: 978-1-4222-3339-9
ISBN: 978-1-4222-3344-3
ebook ISBN: 978-1-4222-8584-8

The Library of Congress has cataloged the hardcopy format(s) as follows:

Library of Congress Cataloging-in-Publication Data

Perritano, John.
  Germany / by John Perritano.
    pages cm. -- (Major nations in a global world: tradition, culture, and daily life)
  Includes index.

  ISBN 978-1-4222-3344-3 (hardback) -- ISBN 978-1-4222-3339-9 (series) -- ISBN 978-1-4222-8584-8 (ebook)
  1. Germany--Juvenile literature. 2. Germany--Social life and customs--Juvenile literature. 3. Germany--Civilization--Juvenile literature. I. Title.
  DD17.P455 2015
  943--dc23
                              2015005027


Developed and produced by MTM Publishing, Inc.
        Project Director        Valerie Tomaselli
        Copyeditor              Lee Motteler/Geomap Corp.
        Editorial Coordinator   Andrea St. Aubin

Indexing Services              Andrea Baron, Shearwater Indexing

Art direction and design by Sherry Williams, Oxygen Design Group

# Contents

Introduction . . . . . . . . . . . . . . . . . . . . . . . . . . 6

**1** History, Religion, and Tradition . . . . . . . . . . . . . . 9

**2** Family and Friends . . . . . . . . . . . . . . . . . . . . . 17

**3** Food and Drink . . . . . . . . . . . . . . . . . . . . . . 25

**4** School, Work, and Industry . . . . . . . . . . . . . . . . 33

**5** Arts and Entertainment . . . . . . . . . . . . . . . . . . 41

**6** Cities, Towns, and the Countryside . . . . . . . . . . . . 49

Further Research . . . . . . . . . . . . . . . . . . . . . . . 56

Series Glossary . . . . . . . . . . . . . . . . . . . . . . . . 57

Index . . . . . . . . . . . . . . . . . . . . . . . . . . . . . 59

Photo Credits . . . . . . . . . . . . . . . . . . . . . . . . . 63

About the Author . . . . . . . . . . . . . . . . . . . . . . . 64

## KEY ICONS TO LOOK FOR:

**Words to Understand:** These words with their easy-to-understand definitions will increase the reader's understanding of the text, while building vocabulary skills.

**Sidebars:** This boxed material within the main text allows readers to build knowledge, gain insights, explore possibilities, and broaden their perspectives by weaving together additional information to provide realistic and holistic perspectives.

**Research Projects:** Readers are pointed toward areas of further inquiry connected to each chapter. Suggestions are provided for projects that encourage deeper research and analysis.

**Text-Dependent Questions:** These questions send the reader back to the text for more careful attention to the evidence presented there.

**Series Glossary of Key Terms:** This back-of-the book glossary contains terminology used throughout this series. Words found here increase the reader's ability to read and comprehend higher-level books and articles in this field.

Medieval Ortenberg Castle at
Baden-Württemberg.

# INTRODUCTION

The Republic of Germany is the seventh largest country in Europe and the continent's most prosperous economy. Although Germany has gone through many transformations in its history, one of its most challenging came when the victorious allied nations of the United States, Great Britain, France, and Soviet Union divided the nation at the end of World War II (1939–1945). The resulting Cold War, an ideological battle between the Western democracies led by the United States and communism, fostered by the Soviet Union, tore German society apart.

Perhaps no one symbol so dramatically illustrated the division than the Berlin Wall, a barrier of concrete watchtowers, razor wire, machine-gun emplacements, bunkers, and guard dogs. The 96-mile (155km) barricade, first built in 1961, separated communist East Berlin and noncommunist West Berlin. For more than forty years, most East Germans suffered under the yoke of communist rule. By the fall of 1989, however, communism was beginning to implode as the liberalizing policies of Soviet Premier Mikhail Gorbachev began to take root. Many Germans believed unification was possible. On November 8, 1989, East Germany announced it would open its border and allow its citizens to travel freely to the West.

The next day, thousands of Berliners flocked to the wall and began slowly dismantling the barrier. Families that hadn't seen each other in decades crossed the border and found joyous celebration in each other's arms. "It was the greatest street party in the history of the world," one journalist said as the jubilant masses sang "*Wir sind ein Volk*—we are one people."

East and West reunited soon after. Germany's rebirth should not come as a surprise, however. The nation has remade itself before.

The Brandenburg Gate and Quadriga statue.

# WORDS TO UNDERSTAND

**barter**: to exchange goods and services in return for other goods and services.

**congress**: an organized group.

**lavish**: opulent; luxurious.

**papal**: relating to the pope or Papacy of the Roman Catholic Church.

# CHAPTER 1

# History, Religion, and Tradition

Although no one knows the exact origins of the first Germanic people, historians say various tribes from across Europe migrated to the region. Located in the middle of the continent, Germany's lack of natural barriers made it easy for foreigners to invade. Julius Caesar realized Germany's vulnerability when he led his Roman legions across the Rhine River in 58–51 BCE. He fought the stubborn tribes he found there and built a series of fortifications along its banks. The Romans then moved eastward toward the Elbe River in 9 CE, but Arminius, a German tribal leader, pushed them back.

Eventually Rome collapsed in the 400s CE, and the disparate Germanic tribes conquered the region Rome once controlled. The tribes then swept across Europe. Some planted the seeds of Christianity, which is still Europe's

A stained-glass church window in the Cologne Cathedral depicts Charlemagne, king of the Franks.

CAROLVS MAGNVS

main religion. Eventually, one of these Christian tribes, the Franks, conquered and united the other tribes, creating a large empire in Germany and part of present-day France.

The Catholic Church had great influence on Germany. On Christmas Day in the year 800, Pope Leo III crowned the king of the Franks, Charlemagne, as western Roman emperor, who ruled much of present-day France and Germany. The Holy Roman Empire, a complicated **congress** of kingdoms, papal states (properties belonging to the Catholic Church), and other smaller territories in western and central Europe, sought to recapture the past glory of Rome as it upheld the ideals of Christianity. After his death, Charlemagne's empire descended into warfare, with each region ruled by its own prince. Otto the Great, a Saxon, suppressed these rebellious regions using the Catholic Church as a stabilizing force.

In 962, the pope crowned Otto the Great Holy Roman emperor. Otto I extended the frontiers of his kingdom. After his death, the empire devolved into war once again as feudal states ruled by petty princes divided Germany. Yet within Germany, the Catholic Church was still a major power with the imperial princes electing the Holy Roman emperor. During the Middle Ages (400s–1300s), these rulers corruptly used the Church to finance a **lavish** lifestyle.

During this period, the Church sold indulgences, which pardoned people for their sins. Many Catholics were angry. They believed the Church was "buying and selling" places in heaven. An ordained monk from Eisleben named Martin Luther was especially critical, not only of the sale of indulgences, but also in the power of the Papacy in present-day Italy. He said the Church and the pope had lost their way. People liked Luther, and he used his intelligence and popularity to take on the powerful Church. He closely studied the Bible and believed its words, not the pope sitting far away in Rome, should influence a person's life.

## BUYING SALVATION

According to the Catholic Church, an indulgence lessened the amount of time a person's soul spent in purgatory, the place where impure souls atoned for their sins on the way to heaven. The Church believed that no one could do enough good deeds to make it to heaven. However, the saints, according to Catholic tradition, had done the heavy lifting for everyone and their surplus of good works was banked in a treasury of sorts. The Church sold access to that treasury. The Church even sold indulgences for those who planned to commit sins in the future.

In 1517, Luther drew up ninety-five theses, or statements, and nailed them to the door of a Catholic Church in Wittenberg. The document stated his grievances with the Church, going well beyond the sale of indulgences. It suggested, to the shock of many, that the popes were naturally limited by God. Luther said the pope had no authority to release souls from purgatory and Christians could be saved from damnation only through their faith.

Church leaders called Luther to appear before the Diet of Worms, an assembly of Church officials, and answer for his actions. (Diet is a formal assembly of officials, and Worms was the city in Germany where the meeting took place.) "Here I stand," Luther supposedly said, "I cannot do otherwise."

Luther refused to retract his statements, and the damage was done. The resulting Protestant Reformation created a cultural, spiritual, and intellectual **upheaval** that split the Catholic Church. Thousands of Catholics formed their own denominations free of **papal** authority. By the end of the Reformation, Lutheranism had

A statue of Martin Luther in Berlin.

Prussia's prime minister Otto von Bismarck was successful in merging parts of Germany and Prussia together, creating a more powerful political union.

become the state religion in Germany and elsewhere. Today there are 800 million Protestants among the planet's 2.2 billion Christians.

By the early 1800s, the Germanic people were still living in a number of small and medium-sized states, as well as in Prussia (in the eastern part of present-day Germany) and in the Austrian Hapsburg Empire. Others had tried to unify these areas but failed. However, Otto von Bismarck, Prussia's prime minister, succeeded in merging the country in 1871, an act that would have tremendous repercussions well into the twentieth century.

### A GERMAN REVOLUTIONARY

Karl Marx was a German philosopher and **revolutionary** socialist born in 1819 in the city of Trier in Prussia. His published *The Communist Manifesto* in 1848. The book sought to explain the goals of Communism. He argued that historical developments revolved around the exploitation of one class over another.

Bismarck believed in the concept of *realpolitik*, the idea that the success of a nation was based using political maneuvering toward realistic goals, not those focused on philosophical or ethical concerns. Today, many people use the term "power politics" to indicate the same approach. Bismarck manipulated German politics to unite the country under Prussian rule. He fought and won wars with Denmark, Austria, and France to unite the thirty-nine independent German states, while adopting liberal social policies at home.

Bismarck's concept of realpolitik influenced Germany long after his death. A system of alliances and treaties with other countries led to German defeat in

World War I (1914–1918). The war, and especially its settlement in the Treaty of Versailles, demoralized and bankrupted the country: under the agreement, Germany was required to pay vast amounts of money in reparations to the victors in the war.

The Great Depression and World War I left Germany broken and tired. There was little to eat and virtually no work. The humiliating Treaty of Versailles, which took away most of Germany's coal and iron production among other things, dashed hopes for any type of economic recovery. There was little the government could do except pay its bills by printing more and more money. That practice eventually forced the German economy toward collapse. By 1932, 6 million Germans could not find jobs. Hitler, like other Germans, blamed the Communists, corrupt businessmen, and Jews for Germany's woes.

Hitler tapped into the hatred and despair that his countrymen were experiencing and formed the Nazi Party. Hitler and the Nazis ultimately led Germany down the path of another more destructive war. The Nazis, who believed themselves pure members of the superior, white Aryan race, rounded up Jews and transported them to concentration camps long before the war had started in 1939. It was part of Hitler's "Final Solution" to rid Europe of Jewish people.

In the end, some 6 million Jews and others, including homosexuals, gypsies, and the "feebleminded," would be systematically murdered.

After the war, power politics played out once again as the victorious nations of the United States, Britain, France, and Soviet Union divided Germany into zones of occupation. The

The signing of the Treaty of Versailles in 1919, securing the end of World War I and the peace settlement that was to cripple Germany's economic prospects and ultimately lead to Hitler's rise and World War II.

Soviet-backed Communists ruled East Germany, while democracy thrived in West Germany. In 1990, a few months after the fall of the Berlin Wall, the East German government collapsed and Germany became one nation again. The country grew to become the world's fourth largest economy and one of the most important players on the world stage.

## POST-WORLD WAR II INTERNATIONAL POLITICS

When the United States, Britain, and the Soviet Union planned to partition Germany into zones of occupation after World War II, the Soviets agreed to declare war against Japan. In return, the Americans and British **bartered** away Eastern Europe, leaving the Soviets—whose army was already there—to dominate those countries.

The Berlin Wall, cutting off the eastern part of the city from the west, in the Tiergarten district in 1988.

A section of the Berlin Wall that remains today.

# TEXT-DEPENDENT QUESTIONS

1. Describe the impact of the Protestant Reformation on the world.

2. How did communism affect East Germany and West Germany?

3. How did Bismarck's use of realpolitik affect Germany in the twentieth century?

# RESEARCH PROJECTS

1. Investigate the life of Martin Luther, focusing specifically on his education and training for the priesthood. Can you draw any conclusions about how his education and training might have led him to break with the Catholic Church? Write a brief essay about your conclusions, making sure to support them with facts about his life.

2. Research communism and capitalism online and create a chart comparing the tenets of the two systems. What can you conclude about the effects of both? Which type of system would you rather live under? Explain your answer.

EIN
FÜRSTENSTAMM,
DESS HELDENLAUF
REICHT BIS
ZU UNSERN TAGEN,
IN GRAUER VORZEIT
GING ER AUF
MIT UNSRES VOLKES
SAGEN.

Portion of the Fuerstenzug mural in Dresden.

Friends drinking punch at a Christmas market.

# WORDS TO UNDERSTAND

**demographics**: the study of population trends.

**marketing**: the process of making products or services desirable to customers.

**Teutonic**: Germanic.

**tumultuous**: involving confusion and disorder.

**wedlock**: the state of being married.

# CHAPTER ⬤2

# Family and Friends

As Germany's place on the world economic stage has grown in recent years, an advertising company, Jung von Matt, in Hamburg set out to find what the "typical German" was thinking. The **marketing** team poured over reams of statistics, survey results, and conducted personal interviews hoping to gauge the likes, dislikes, hates, and prejudices of the average German.

From this data, a fictional couple emerged, a make-believe husband and wife named Thomas and Sabine Müller. The Müllers quickly became a sort of **Teutonic** everyman and everywoman. Politicians, grocery store owners, car dealers, and others wanted to know what Thomas and Sabine were thinking;

what they were buying, what they were eating, and what their favorite car color was (it was first red, then changed to gray, and then again to black).

Thomas and Sabine also had an extraordinarily high regard for family and friends, although Thomas thought slightly more of his family than Sabine thought of hers. In fact, the Müllers, like the majority of Germans, placed family first in their lives.

---

## THE AVERAGE GERMAN LIVING ROOM

The company Jung von Matt's "creation" of the average German couple, Thomas and Sabine Müller, is embodied in a live model in the company's Hamburg headquarters of what their living room might look like. The walls are painted yellow, for instance, and the pictures they hang on the walls are of family and animals. Reading material in the room includes volumes in the Harry Potter series and a travel guide to a Mediterranean island.

---

While immigrants from other nations, including Turkey, Syria, Iraq, and the Balkans, have changed the face of Germany, family is still central to German culture. In fact, the newcomers have also brought a strong sense of family with

Friends and family enjoy the afternoon in the Marktplatz in the old town of Berchtesgaden.

them. The Turks first came to Germany looking for work as "guest workers." Once they were settled, they encouraged their extended family members to move to Germany. Now, the first Turkish teachers born in Germany are teaching in schools, and even Turkish actors have broken into German television.

Family is still a strong part of the social structure in Germany.

While there's no doubt Germans place a high value on family, the makeup of the German family has changed dramatically in recent decades. The traditional German family—a married couple with children where the father is the sole provider and the mother takes care of the home—is slowly becoming an a thing of the past.

In 2014, 21 percent of German households were headed by a woman, while nearly 25 percent were made up of married couples without children. Slightly less than 33 percent of the population is made up of adults with children in the home. Moreover, about 65 percent of mothers and 70 percent of working-age women are employed outside the house, while one in five women between the ages of forty and forty-four has never had a child.

Moreover, out-of-**wedlock** births are another indication that Germany is moving away from the traditional concept of family. In the late 1980s, about 12 percent of women in West Germany and East Germany gave birth to babies outside of marriage. That figure has grown to 30 percent in 2011.

Interestingly, the percentage of children born outside of marriage in eastern Germany is much higher than the west: 57 percent compared to 25 percent. No one can pinpoint why that is, however. Some researchers suspect that the family policies of communist East Germany, which offered more help to unwed mothers than West Germany, might be a factor. Although Germany's **demographics** are constantly shifting and the average size of the German household is in decline, the importance of family has increased rather than decreased. Seventy-two percent of twelve to twenty-five year olds say their happiness is dependent on their family, while 90 percent of all Germans say family always comes first.

The Christmas market in Frankfurt epitomizes the pleasures of holiday celebrations in Germany.

Such emphasis on family is remarkable in a society that has undergone a number of **tumultuous** political, sociological, and economic upheavals during the past century. As the country has evolved, so have family relations. Those relationships are now based on involvement, affection, independence, and equal rights, not on the timeworn concepts of obedience, subordination, and dependence.

Part of the reason Germany is so family-centric is the country's shared cultural heritage. And no traditions have more meaning to the German people then those involving Christmas, or Weihnachten. In fact, the traditions are sometimes more important than Christmas itself. The season is a way for families and friends to connect.

## CHRISTMAS TREE LEGENDS

Legend says that the first use of an evergreen tree to celebrate the holiday was in the 1500s when Martin Luther brought a fir tree into his house and lit it up by tying candles around the boughs, but this has not been proven by historians. Some say that Christmas trees had their roots in the German "miracle plays," plays put on to teach peasants Bible stories, of the Middle Ages. A decorated evergreen tree was placed in the middle of the stage to represent the tree of life. Whatever the exact details, it seems certain that the first use of an evergreen at Christmas time can be traced to Alsace, the western region of present-day Germany.

The celebrations begin during Advent, the four-week period before Christmas Day. To mark the period, most German households have an Advent wreath made up of four purple candles and one white. The family lights a purple candle every Sunday, while the white candle, which symbolizes the birth of Christ, is lit close to midnight on Christmas Eve. The importance of Christmas can also be seen in the massive Christmas markets in the cities, towns, and villages. These markets are where thousands gather to buy food, gifts, and to share in the Yuletide cheer.

Germany's wedding traditions are also important to personal relationships. The typical traditional wedding—still practiced by some couples, especially in the countryside—is a three-day affair. The couple is married first by a justice of the peace, known as a *stadesbeamte*. It is illegal for a couple to be married in a church-only ceremony. Nevertheless, a huge party, the *polterabend*, or "the evening with lots of broken porcelain," is held the day after the civil ceremony. Friends and relatives bring porcelain plates and smash them in front of the couple.

Having salt bread and drinking schnapps is a German wedding tradition.

## BREAKING DISHES BRINGS GOOD LUCK!

The tradition *polterabend*—friends and family members smashing plates in honor of the bride and bridegroom at a reception—is supposed to bestow good luck on the bride and groom. The couple, however, is responsible for the cleanup.

At the beginning of the church service, the bride and groom walk down the aisle together. At the end of the ceremony, people throw rice at the departing couple. The Germans believe the bride will have as many children as there are grains of rice in her hair. In turn, the couple tosses coins for children to catch.

Finally, another reception is held. This time friends "kidnap" the bride and bring her to a local pub, the location of which is kept secret from the groom. When the groom finally finds his wife, he is obligated to pay for the drinks.

Like family, friends are important to the German people. For them, the concept of friendship is different than the concept of friendship in the United States. Americans will often say they have many friends, but their relationships are often loose. On the other hand, Germans have a tight group of friends. Friendships are not made quickly in Germany, but they do last for life. In the United States, Americans often form friendships at work, while Germans, especially those that are older, are more likely to keep their private and work life separate.

## GATHERING AT EASTERTIME

Easter is a very important holiday in Germany for family and friends. On the eve of Easter Sunday, people gather around raging bonfires that use old Christmas trees as a source of fuel. It is a pagan ritual symbolizing the coming of spring.

A Christmas tree ablaze on the eve of Easter Sunday in Graal-Mueritz located in the northeast on the Baltic Sea.

# TEXT-DEPENDENT QUESTIONS

1.  Name two ways the Germany family unit has changed in recent years.

2.  How do modern German families maintain their sense of relevance even though the demographics are shifting?

3.  Describe how German wedding traditions underscore the closeness of relationships.

# RESEARCH PROJECTS

1. Research some of the differences between the wedding traditions in the United States and wedding traditions in Germany. How are they different? How are they alike?

2. Review the article "A Day in the Life: What Makes the Average German Tick?" available at this link (http://www.spiegel.de/international/germany/a-day-in-the-life-what-makes-the-average-german-tick-a-550107.html) to learn more about the fictional average German couple, Thomas and Sabine Müller. Write a short report—three to four paragraphs—about any additional aspect of their lives that interests you.

Friends in a beer garden in Bavaria.

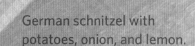
German schnitzel with
potatoes, onion, and lemon.

# WORDS TO UNDERSTAND

**antiquity**: ancient history.

**conform**: to think or behave in a socially acceptable or expected way.

**corpulent**: pudgy; plump.

**gastronomic**: relating to food.

**mosaic**: a type of visual art made of small, often multicolored stones.

**seismic**: great or extremely large.

# CHAPTER ⬤3

# Food and Drink

It wasn't that long ago that the stereotype of Germans subsisting on a diet of sausages, potatoes, and sauerkraut was common. Cartoons often showed plump Germans stuffing their **corpulent** faces with sausages and swilling beer from overflowing steins. The days of sausages and beer might not be totally gone, but the country's cuisine, like Germany itself, has undergone a **seismic** transformation in recent decades, a shift fueled by immigrants who have brought their own culinary traditions to Germany.

The newcomers, especially from the Mediterranean, began flocking to Germany in the 1960s. They opened restaurants and food stores, including those catering to Greek, Italian, and Turkish tastes. The Germans themselves have also had a hand in this culinary shift. Many people travel widely between countries, and when they do, they often bring back exotic recipes. Moreover, the opening of trade barriers (thanks to Germany's admission to the European Union) allows more imported goods to flow into the country. Supermarket shelves brim with foodstuffs, fruits, and vegetables from other countries.

## STREET VENDOR SANDWICH

The *döner kebap* sandwich, which consists of baked pita bread filled with roasted meat and topped with lettuce, tomato, onions, and other vegetables, is one of the most popular street foods in Germany. Supposedly, the sandwich, which is sold by street vendors, was first made in Berlin by a Turkish immigrant named Mahmut Aygun.

The result has been a **mosaic** of food that tantalizes the most discriminating Teutonic tastes. Although the diet of younger Germans is much healthier than in previous generations, many Germans still crave sausage, dumplings, potato pancakes, and other traditional eats. Sausage—and it comes in many varieties—is probably the most important strand of the country's **gastronomic** web. While these tasty links of meat mixed with spices wrapped in animal casings have been around since **antiquity**, the German sausage is a work of culinary art. From Bavaria to the North Sea, sausage is served in many forms. In fact, most critics would be hard pressed to find a better tasting sausage than those made in Germany.

Sausages have an important place in Germany's history, with each region creating its own delectable version. In the southern region of Bavaria, which is greatly influenced by Austrian cooking, diners often find hearty meals made from simple ingredients, such as knödel, or dumplings,

Sliced potatoes are a delicious complement to Nuremberg bratwurst.

and a sausage called *weiss-wurst*. A combination of pork spiced with bacon, onions, pepper, lemon-powder, and parsley, the weisswurst is white in color with a mild taste.

Legend has it that the first weisswurst was stuffed by a Munich butcher named Joseph Moser in 1857. Moser was try-

Potato dumplings stuffed with minced sausage are often served with sauerkraut.

ing to make bratwurst—another type of sausage—but ran out of ingredients. He milled about his kitchen and filled the casings with what he had. He boiled his meaty creation fearing that grilling would split them open. People ate it up.

In the south-central state of Franconia near the city of Nuremberg, the Nuremberg bratwurst, made from pork and seasoned with marjoram, salt, pepper, and other spices, is popular. The early sausage makers of Franconia were required to have experts judge their brats. Each link had to **conform** to certain standards, including the use of ingredients, overall quality, and water content.

Butchers cried foul. Such oversight, they complained, made it expensive to make the sausage. Finally, the butchers came up with a solution. They made the bratwurst smaller and thinner. They sold tons of them and were able to stay in business. These days, sizzling Nuremberg brats are served six, eight, ten, and twelve at a time, along with a side of horseradish, sauerkraut, white cabbage, red cabbage, turnips, or potatoes.

## THE LITTLE DOG

Germany can take credit for inventing the most popular sausage of all—the hot dog. The Germans call it the "dachshund" or "little dog." The first little dog, some say, was made by a butcher named Johann Georghehner in the 1600s, although no one really knows for sure. That's because the origins of the hot dog are murky. Those living in Frankfurt say the hot dog, or "frankfurter," was invented there in 1487. Those living in Vienna, Austria, say the "wiener" was first cooked up in their city. Eventually someone put the hot dog on a bun.

Yet, German cuisine is much more than sausage, sauerkraut, or potatoes. In northwestern Germany, close to the North and Baltic seas, seafood is plentiful. In Hamburg, Germany's second largest city, fish, crab, eel, and lobster are among the favorite dishes.

In Bremen, also in the north, whose harbor is the second largest German port for foreign cargo ships, exotic imported ingredients spice meals. Those living in the region also enjoy potatoes and kale, a cabbage-like vegetable. Kale is so important that many communities hold kale festivals and take part in *kohlfahrten*, or kale tours. The tours consist of long hikes in the local countryside that end in a dinner of kale, sausage, and schnapps, an alcoholic beverage.

Germans also love their bread and, according to many sources, have 200 kinds to choose from. Some of the most popular are pumpernickel, which is dark and heavy; *roggenbrot*, a rye bread made from sourdough; and *leinsamenbrot*, another type of rye bread.

If sausages are the quintessential German food, then beer is the quintessential German drink. Beer informs many aspects of life. Centuries ago, beer was considered a type of health food that kept people from getting sick. At the time, drinking water could kill you. Beer, however, was good because the brewing process killed the pathogens that made people ill. Beer making was one of the first things European settlers brought to the New World in the seventeenth century.

Kale is an important part of northern German cuisine; some communities even sponsor their own kale festivals and *kohlfahrten*, or kale tours.

In northwestern Germany, bordering the North Sea, fish markets like this one are popular. They were originally open before church on Sunday morning and sold their seafood directly from fishing boats.

A wide array of bread on display in a bakery in Aachen, the westernmost town in the country, on the border with the Netherlands and Belgium. There are supposedly 200 types of bread to choose from in Germany.

No one brewed beer better than the Germans. In the 1500s, the Germans drank ale that was mostly brewed by professionals, including monks and nuns. In 1516, Bavarian noblemen passed a law stating that German beer should include only hops, barely, water, and no other ingredients. Yeast was added to the list centuries later. Known as the Reinheitsgebot, the law is one of the oldest food and beverage laws in the world. Although the intent of the Reinheitsgebot was to make sure there were enough crops to make bread, it quickly became associated with high-quality beer. Many brewers still abide by the rule.

Local communities have always taken pride in the quality of their brews. People often know where a person comes from by the type of beer they drink. Germans have devoted songs to beer drinking. Strangers share long tables in beer halls and beer gardens, joining arms and singing with their steins full of the amber liquid. In some places, beer drinkers still participate in the custom of "boot drinking" or *stiefeltrinken*, in which a glass boot holding about four pints of beer is passed around a large table. Each person gulps from the boot.

Perhaps no culinary tradition best captures the spirit of the country than the modern Oktoberfest, where beer and sausage

Wheat beers, both light and dark, are popular in Germany.

Oktoberfest in Munich in 2007. Festivalgoers drink more than 1 million gallons of beer across Germany during the typical fall festivities!

meet in an annual celebration that begins in late September and lasts until the first Sunday in October. The festivities are held to commemorate the 1810 marriage of Bavarian Crown Prince Ludwig to the Princess Therese. Each year in Munich, Oktoberfest celebrants consume more than 1 million gallons of beer, 200,000 pounds of pork sausage, and 480,000 roasted chickens. The festival has been transported to other parts of the world with large German immigrant populations. In the United States, one of the biggest is in Cincinnati, Ohio, and Oktoberfest in Canada's twin cities of Waterloo and Kirchener, in the southeast near Toronto, is considered the largest outside of Germany.

## LEGENDS OF A CAKE

German chocolate cake does not come from Germany. In 1852, an American named Sam German invented a sweet chocolate baking bar for the Baker's Chocolate Co. in Dorchester, Massachusetts. The company named the bar "Baker's German's Sweet Chocolate." The first-known printed recipe for the cake was published in 1957 in a Dallas newspaper and it said to use German's Sweet Chocolate. Afterward there was a spike in the sale of the bar, and the recipe was reprinted in many more newspapers. Eventually, the tasty recipe became known as German chocolate cake.

# TEXT-DEPENDENT QUESTIONS

1. How has Germany's culinary heritage changed over the decades?

2. What role does beer play in Germany's identity?

3. Why did Bavarian officials pass the Reinheitsgebot?

# RESEARCH PROJECTS

1. Research and write an essay on how immigrants influenced the types of food Germans eat today.

2. Gather three or four sausage recipes from different countries. Compare the ingredients in each recipe. Are they different? If so, why do you think they're different? Explain whether these recipes mirror that country's culinary heritage.

German pretzels.

A state-of-the-art brewery in Germany.

# WORDS TO UNDERSTAND

**ample**: more than enough.

**dominate**: to have control, power, or authority over someone or something.

**emulate**: an attempt to equal or surpass somebody or something that is successful.

**mediocre**: average or below average.

**obligated**: compelled to do something.

# CHAPTER 4

# School, Work, and Industry

Education and industrial might have always been hallmarks of German life. The country is known for its great scientists, its great automobiles, and its rigorous educational system. Universities and colleges around the globe have always sought to **emulate** Germany's successful universities. Many countries, especially in Europe, look with envy on the German economy that now **dominates** the continent.

Part of Germany's success has been the country's standard-setting educational system, especially its universities. Scientists such as Albert Einstein, Max Planck, and Gustav Hertz were all products of Germany's educational system. Because of this focus on education, the country has a 99 percent literacy rate, while 86 percent of adults, ages twenty-five to sixty-four, have earned a high school degree or equivalent.

Parents give their children cardboard cornets filled with sweets and small presents on their first day of school to celebrate the milestone.

Each state, or land, and not the federal government, is responsible for education at the primary and university level. The states, each in their own way, hold students to extraordinarily high standards, although those standards are nothing like the outdated and extremely strict Prussian system that produced many notable intellectuals.

### A MEDIOCRE STUDENT

Perhaps the most famous German student was Albert Einstein, a great thinker and scientist whose discoveries changed the way we view the universe. Born in the city of Ulm in 1879, Einstein was given a compass by his father when he was around ten years old. The young Einstein was so fascinated by the unseen forces that made the needle move that he began a life-long quest of education. Einstein was a **mediocre** student at best (he never failed math as some claim), but he had an **ample** curiosity.

While each of the sixteen states has different academic goals, they generally focus on traditional courses, such as math and language, with arts instruction, such as music and photography, taking a back seat. All länders require that children over the age of six attend four years of primary school, known as *grundschule* (or basic school). Once they leave *grundschule*, usually in the fourth year, students are **obligated** to attend a secondary school. In Germany, there are four main types of secondary schools, each with different curricula and standards. The gymnasium is the most difficult of the group. Children usually enroll at gymnasium at about the age of twelve and stay until they are eighteen or nineteen years old. Those wishing to go to a university attend gymnasium, where they are obligated to take two foreign languages.

*Realschule* is an intermediate secondary school that offers general and vocational education. After sixteen years of school, those graduating *hauptschule* generally go on to attend a vocational school as they learn a trade. Many of the länders also run schools known as *gesamtschule*, which is a union of the other schools, where students from the fifth through the eleventh grades advance to more demanding courses based on their ability.

In Germany, high school graduates attend traditional university, or *universitäten*, or universities of applied science (*fachhochschulen* or *hochschulen*). Ten percent of Germany's college students come from other countries. About

Founded in 1810, the Humboldt University of Berlin is one of city's oldest universities.

43 percent of high school students attend college, which is paid for by the state except in five länders. Students generally spend three years to achieve a bachelor's degree and two additional years to graduate with a master's degree.

The focus on higher education has helped Germany become the world's fourth largest economy in a relatively short period since unification in 1990. But unification posed many vexing problems for the new German economy. West Germany had the strongest economy, and it had to absorb tens of thousands of workers from East Germany and provide them with good wages and benefits. The nation struggled at first, but slowly things began to change. Factories, such as Volkswagen, began to churn out products. Good-paying jobs became plentiful.

 **FORWARD-THINKING STRATEGIES**

Although Germany is an economic powerhouse, it is reliant on other countries for much of its energy resources, especially those from fossil fuels such as oil and natural gas. Consequently, Germany has begun to develop renewable energy, which now accounts for over 25 percent of the energy consumed in the country.

In 1999, Germany joined the European Union, which provided Germans with a common market to sell their wares. In fact, Germany is Europe's leading automaker, engineering such high-quality cars as Volkswagen, Mercedes-Benz, BMW, and Porsche. In fact, it was two Germans, Karl Friedrick Benz and Gottlieb Daimler, whom historians say were the first to file patents for a gasoline-powered automobile on January 29, 1886, in two different German cities. Benz's model had three wheels, which he first drove in 1885; Daimler's car was the first four-wheel auto.

Today, German passenger cars account for 17 percent of the global market, helping to make car manufacturing the most important industry in Germany. Car manufacturing represents 20 percent of Germany's industrial

The hyper-modern BMW Welt, an exhibition center at BMW's headquarters in Munich, which opened in 2007.

A train running on the tracks along the Moselle River.

Container ships navigate the Elbe River in the Hamburg Harbor.

revenue. Germany also sells many cars overseas. Around 77 percent of German-made automobiles were built for export in 2011.

The Airbus A380 super jumbo jet, the world's largest passenger airplane, and Frankfurt's International Airport, which is the size of 2,000 football fields, also scream success. Built partly in Germany, the A380 flies in and out of the Frankfurt airport, which was expanded to receive the impressive passenger plane. In Hamburg, headquarters of Airbus in Germany, 15,000 workers design and engineer the plane. The factory also houses the component assembly hall, which assembles the A380's fuselage.

Part of Germany's economic success can also be traced to its social-market economy, a form of capitalism in which the government protects the competitive environment from monopolies, while also protecting consumers, workers, and others. Germany's expansive highway system, canal system, and railroads have also had a hand in the country's economic success. These transportation systems link every part of the country, allowing companies to move goods from one corner of Europe to another.

Globalization, which has increased the economic ties among countries, has also helped make Germany Europe's richest nation and a world leader in iron, steel, and coal production. German companies export electronics, chemicals, and automobiles. Globalization has allowed Germany to connect with its neighbors and others to help fuel trade.

## FACTORIES IN THE RUHR

German's main industrial areas include those in Ruhr district in North Rhine-Westphalia. It is rich with coal mines that fuel the multitude of factories in the area. Factories are also concentrated around several large cities, including Munich and Stuttgart.

But with success comes problems. Germany now has too few workers and too many jobs, a situation that is only going to get worse because the country's population is aging. Twenty percent of Germany's population is sixty-five years or older, while the median age is forty-five years old. Experts say that by 2020, Germany will need about 2 million people to fill open jobs.

To increase the size of its workforce, Germany opened its borders to immigrant workers. Years ago, Germany stopped foreigner workers from coming into the country. Many feared the immigrants would take jobs away from native Germans. These days, Germany's door is wide open as people from Eastern Europe pour into the country to fill open positions, especially those in the health and engineering professions, and people from further east, such as Turkey, fill jobs in the service sector.

The blast furnaces of the steel mills of Duisburg, a city located in the industrial Ruhr area in Germany's far west. The Ruhr is the country's largest steel-producing center.

# TEXT-DEPENDENT QUESTIONS

1. Which part of Germany is known for its vast coal reserves?
2. Which school prepares students for university study?
3. What are the levels of schooling in Germany?

# RESEARCH PROJECT

Go to your school parking lot or the parking lot of a mall or shopping center and count the number of cars made in Germany and the number of cars made by other foreign countries, such as Japan and South Korea. When you're finished, create a bar chart to represent your findings.

Mercedes Benz GLA-Class at the Automobile International Trade Fair in 2014.

The Bauhaus Building, designed by Walter Gropius in 1926–1927.

# WORDS TO UNDERSTAND

**boisterous**: noisy and enthusiastic.

**encompass**: to include or envelop something.

**inspiration**: stimulation for a person to be creative.

**reverberate**: to become filled with.

# CHAPTER  5

# Arts and Entertainment

The streets of Berlin were a sea of clapping hands and outstretched arms. Thousands of soccer fans, some waving the national flag, crowded the city's boulevards after the German national soccer team won the 2014 World Cup in Brazil. With so many cheering, screaming Germans, the celebration nearly rivaled the fall of the Berlin Wall.

A couple of days later, hundreds of thousands stood shoulder to shoulder to welcome the team home with a parade. Nearly half a million fans packed Berlin's "fan mile," a street that runs west of the capital to the Brandenburg Gate. Many arrived the night before hoping to carve out a special spot to see the parade.

"We're all world champions," one of the players later shouted to a cascade of applause and cheering. The 1-0 win over Argentina in Rio de Janeiro was the first World Cup victory in the reunited Germany, although West Germany had won the event in 1954, 1974, and 1990. Many who attended the event painted their faces black, red, and gold—Germany's national colors.

The celebration underscored the love affair Germans have with soccer. Yet, soccer is one facet of Germany's rich arts and entertainment culture, which **encompasses** everything from dance clubs and classical music to wine festivals and Oktoberfest.

## STAYING UP TIL DAWN

Berlin has a vibrant nightlife with many different types of dance clubs and cafés. People from around the country, and the world, come to Berlin to dance to the beat of hip-hop, disco, and other types of live music. The club scene is known for its late hours and out-of-the-way, underground feel.

Fans in Berlin celebrate the German soccer team at the end of the 2006 World Cup hosted by Germany.

Music lovers gather to celebrate the music of Johann Sebastian Bach at Bachfest in Leipzig, the musician's home town.

Yet, sports resonate with many young Germans, and older ones, too. In recent years, Germany has exploded with playing fields, fitness centers, swimming pools, and Olympic training facilities. While sports such as basketball and hockey are popular, soccer is king. The country is dotted with thousands of amateur soccer clubs. Professional games draw an average 25,000 fans.

Germany was also home to many world-class tennis players, such as s Boris Becker, Steffi Graf, Anke Huber, and Michael Stich. Formula One (F1) racing is immensely popular, thanks in part to Michael Schumacher, who was one of the top-earning F1 drivers in the world. He made about $80 million in 2004 and had more victories and won more championships during his career than any other racer.

If Germans love sports, they adore music, especially its classic form. Classical music has always been central to German life. Only a few other countries, notably Italy, Austria, and France, can compete with German classical music. The country's large cities nurtured some of the best European composers, including Handel and Bach, Beethoven and Brahms, Schumann and Schütz, Wagner and Hindemith.

The country's love affair with classical music **reverberates** today. Many cities celebrate the lives of Germany's great musicians with musical festivals. One of the most popular is Bachfest Leipzig, which is held every year in the city where Johann Sebastian Bach lived and worked from 1720 until he died thirty years later. The city began hosting the festival in 1904.

Not to be outdone, the Bayreuth Opera Festival comes alive each July and August with the music and operas of Richard Wagner, the nineteenth-century composer. Wagner actually helped design the Bayreuth Festspilhaus, or Bayreuth Festival Theater, located just north of the city, much to the dismay of the original architect. Wagner constantly changed the design. The festival is a must-see for Wagner fans that have no problem paying for pricy tickets.

While classical music rocks, Germany is also a bastion of contemporary music. The locals in Hamburg like to think of their city as a rock 'n' roll heaven, where one of the greatest rock groups in history, the Beatles, honed their talents. The residents of Hamburg might be on to something. It could be that the city's eclectic music scene is fueled by Hamburg's harbor, bringing different cultures together in one spot. Or, perhaps it is the street-wise, hardworking, grittiness of Hamburg's neighborhoods that give local bands their edge. Whatever the reason, people travel thousands of miles to take part in Hamburg's music scene, especially when they come to see the Reeperbahn Festival, which draws performers from the worlds of pop, indie, rock, electro, hip-hop, soul, and jazz music.

 **THE BEATLES IN GERMANY**

It was in Hamburg that the Beatles, who many regard as the best rock 'n' roll band in history, polished their style and their music. Their first performance was at the Indra Club in a not-so-nice section of the city. Over the next two years, their band would play 281 concerts in Hamburg. In 1961, they played ninety-eight straight nights. "It was our apprenticeship," Harrison said. Best and Sutcliffe would eventually leave the Beatles.

Sometimes though, people prefer a more traditional form of music. In the Alpine regions, such as Bavaria and elsewhere, visitors can often hear the folk songs of *volksmusick*, or "people's music." The term describes the union

This 1988 German stamp depicts Beatles musician John Lennon.

Members of a local dancing group dance the famous Schuhplattler at a folk festival in Bavaria.

of traditional music from Germany, Austria, Switzerland, and other Alpine locations. Central to *volksmusick* are alpenhorns, long wooden horns with cup-shaped mouthpieces; zithers, thin, flat-bodied stringed instruments; violas and harmonicas.

The customs of each German region can be seen in the country's style of dance. Upbeat polkas, solemn waltzes, and **boisterous** country dances all reflect bits of German regional life. The Ländler, for example, is a couple's dance that originated in Bavaria and Austria. Couples dance to a lively tune, which allows them turn in each other's arms. For the most part, folk dancers follow strict gender roles. Males stomp and clap, while females twirl with their skirts in the air, their legs kicking high.

Germany is also a center for art, which explains why one of the most popular art exhibitions in Great Britain in 2014 was a show put on by German artist Anselm Kiefer. Critics and experts say Kiefer is one of world's most imaginative and serious artists in the world. Raised along the Rhine in the Black Forest, Kiefer had planned from childhood to become an artist. In fact, he was named for Anselm Feuerbach, one of Germany's top nineteenth-century painters.

Kiefer draws his **inspiration** from German history, its myth, its literature, and its folk customs. Kiefer is not the only heavyweight artist from Germany. The abstract paintings of Gerhard Richter have been prominently displayed in

The 1862 painting, oil on canvas, titled *Iphigenie* by Anselm Feuerbach, one of Germany's premier artists of the nineteenth century.

such well-known places as the Museum of Modern Art in New York City.

Although Richter had been painting for decades, he painted his most famous work recently, an abstract study of the terrorist attack against the World Trade Center in New York City on September 11, 2001. For many, the painting was sad, yet it captured the enormity of the event. It's "the closest you will get to a great 9/11 work," one critic, Brian Appleyard, wrote. "It reclaims the day, leaving it exactly where it was, exactly when it happened."

Most Germans probably don't go to a museum to muse about art, but most watch TV. Television in Germany is dominated, as it is in other countries, by reality shows including modeling and singing competitions. One of the most watched shows in Germany is "Wetten Dass...?" a competition show in which contestants accept crazy challenges. People often call the show, with its 10 million viewers, the biggest TV program in Europe. "Wetten Dass...?" which loosely translates into "Want to Bet That . . . ?" has been around for more than thirty years. Contestants bet on accomplishing strange feats.

## A TV SHOW'S POPULARITY

Although popular, "Wetten Dass . . . ?" has faced criticism. In 2010, a young male contestant was paralyzed from the neck down when he tried to jump over a speeding car while on spring-loaded stilts. The car was driven by the man's father. Millions of viewers watched the mishap. Critics say the show, which is funded by Germany's two public television stations, debases German culture. The popularity of "Want to Bet That . . . ?" has waned in the past several years. At its peak, 23 million viewers watched.

# TEXT-DEPENDENT QUESTIONS

1. Which team did Germany beat in the 2014 World Cup?

2. In which city did the Beatles perform when they were teenagers?

3. How many viewers watched "Wetten Dass...?" during the height of its popularity?

# RESEARCH PROJECTS

1. Use the Internet and the library to research and create a computerized slide-show timeline of major highlights in German music history.

2. Pick one of the German artists mentioned in the text and create a visual scrapbook of that person's work. Write a caption alongside the pictures that describes each of the paintings.

3. Find a list of German reality TV shows and compare them to a list of American reality shows. Write down the differences and the similarities between shows.

German heavy metal band Bonfire.

A Bavarian farmhouse in southern Germany.

## WORDS TO UNDERSTAND

**fertile**: an area that is good for farming, where crops can grow.

**navigable**: passable by ship or boat.

**quaint**: with a charming, old-fashioned quality.

**spire**: a tall, pointed structure on the top of a roof, tower, or steeple.

# CHAPTER **6**

# Cities, Towns, and the Countryside

When you think of Germany, what comes to mind? Is it the Alpine villages near the Swiss border? Is it the medieval castles on the Rhine? Is it the gothic **spires** of a Hamburg church? Germany might seem mysterious, but it really isn't. The country is not only marked with verdant, yet dark and seemingly foreboding forests, but also craggy mountain peaks that tickle the clouds and cobblestone villages and sturdy hamlets that have inspired fairy tales and have withstood the ravages of an often violent history.

Indeed, the variety of German landscapes is startling in a country less than 5 percent the size of the United States. The lush hillsides of Franconia in northern Bavaria are home to many well-preserved medieval castles, churches, and

Kayakers on Lake Constance in Konstanz, in western Germany, where historic houses line the banks of the lake.

monasteries. Flowing out of the Alps, the tributaries of the Danube River slowly build up force in Franconia. The Danube runs so deep by the time it reaches the Austrian border that commercial ships have no problem plying its waters.

## A BAVARIAN CHRISTMAS MARKET

The Christmas market, or Christkindlesmarkt, is a familiar wintertime feature in many towns throughout Germany. The Nuremberg Christmas market begins late in November and runs until Christmas Eve. It is one of the oldest and largest Christmas markets in Germany, although not the only one in Bavaria.

Southwest of Franconia in Baden-Württemberg near the border with Switzerland is one of the most popular vacation spots in Germany—Lake Constance. Lake Constance is on the Rhine River and is the third largest lake in Germany. The hillsides around the lake are dotted with orchards, vineyards, and **quaint** villages and hamlets. The 160-mile (260-km) lake is shared by Austria, Germany, and Switzerland.

One of the greatest rivers on the European continent is the nearly 800-mile Rhine River. The river is not only a scenic wonder but serves as an important transportation artery. The Rhine has played a major role in Germany's history and cultural unification. The Rhine begins flowing as a violent stream out of the

Swiss Alps down to the North Sea in the Netherlands. The river is **navigable** for nearly 500 miles (805 km) from the North Sea to the city of Basel in Switzerland. Oceangoing ships can enter the river near Rotterdam in the Netherlands and make their way south to Cologne in Germany.

Sailing the Rhine on one of the many river barges is a time machine back to the past. Look to your right and you can see medieval castles built by feudal lords to protect their land. Look to your left and your eyes will be treated to vineyard-covered hillsides and even more castles and fortresses. Some of the oldest vineyards in the Rhineland date back to the time of the Romans. In fact, most German vineyards are located in the **fertile** river valley.

## DARK WOODS

Legends of sorcerers and wizards, dwarves and wolves all make the Black Forest perhaps one of the spookiest spots on the planet. Running parallel to the Rhine, the pine- and spruce-filled forest teems with macabre and supernatural stories handed down from generation to generation. The name comes from the Romans, who thought the trees that filled the forest looked black.

A roofed bridge sits above the Forbach River in the northern part of the Black Forest.

Quedlinburg, in central Germany, one of the country's historic villages that escaped the destruction of World War II.

Also along the river's banks are sleepy villages, but that's not uncommon in Germany. Many Germany villages have withstood the destruction of a violent history that includes two world wars. To walk down their quaint streets is like being transported to an ancient and medieval land.

Such is the case in Quedlinburg, located close to the center of the country in Saxony-Anhalt. World War II mostly bypassed the town nestled in the Harz Mountains, allowing the burg to keep its medieval flavor and architecture. The town owes its wealth and prestige to Henry I, a German king who encouraged his subjects to build towns and cities. When Henry died in 936, his widow remained in Quedlinburg, living at the collegiate church of St. Servatius on Castle Hill, which overlooks the community. Unwed mothers of the nobility later used the church as a college. Below Castle Hill, visitors can wander down cobblestone streets to see the elaborately timber-framed houses first built in the 1500s and 1600s.

Although one can be magically transported to the past in such places, it is important to note that Germany's rural landscape and environment is a far cry from what it used to be. It only takes a short drive from any one town to reach an autobahn, or highway, and from there, the spires of Germany's gleaming modern cities. The autobahn connects all corners of Germany, a nearly 7,000-mile (11,260-km) highway whose asphalt tentacles reach from the Baltic to Bavaria, from the Rhine to Brandenburg, and all points in between. Construction of the first autobahn (its official name is Bundesautobahn) between Cologne and Boon began in 1929 and ended in 1932.

While picturesque villages are seemingly everywhere, it is Germany's cities that are now the hub of culture, history, and economic life. As in other countries, people are moving out of the countryside and into the cities, draining the rural areas of people and money.

## IN A NEW LAND

Immigrants from Turkey have influenced Germany and its cities for many years now. The Turks first came during the 1960s as "guest workers" when the labor shortage in Germany began. Forming the largest ethnic minority in the country, with nearly 2.7 million people, they have influenced German culture greatly—especially the cuisine and pop culture scene, and Turkish students fill Germany's universities.

Perhaps there is no more symbolic a city in all of Germany, or Europe for that matter, as Berlin, home to world-famous museums, theaters, monuments, and interesting neighborhoods with diverse nightlife. Berlin is an emotional city, a key player in Germany's unification, two world wars, the Cold War, and reunification. Nowhere can this emotion be felt more than in the city's architecture. The cityscape mixes remnants of Old World and New, communism and social democracy, prosperity and poverty. And no landmark more than the Berlin Wall is the ultimate symbol of the country's recent political history. Parts of the wall that still exist have morphed into open-air galleries where art mixes with political and social commentary.

Berlin, a bustling cultural center, merging its old and new architecture and a vibrant art and music scene.

The Neuschwanstein Castle in Bavaria appears to be straight out of a fairy tale.

The university city has always been an important part of Germany, and no city better fits into that role than Heidelberg. Located in the north of Baden-Württtenberg, Heidelberg is home to the University of Heidelberg, the oldest university in Germany.

Like many of Germany's university cities, Heidelberg is a blend of the old and the new. Overlooking the city with a population of 143,000 are the ruins of Heidelberg Castle, an imposing structure that historians say is the most important building of the Renaissance north of the Alps. Construction of the castle began in 1214, and today this palace of kings and prison of popes spies down on the countryside. Heidelberg today is the center of a robust biotechnology industry and research institutes including the Max Planck Institutes. (Max Planck was a theoretical physisist who won the Nobel Prize in Physics in 1918 for his theories on quantum physics.)

Leipzig, home of Leipzig University in eastern Germany, was once a dreary town when it was under Communist rule. Today the city is one of the liveliest in Germany, energized by the 20,000 students who live there and the high-tech industries that have opened shop. Surrounding the city is a belt of parks and gardens.

## FAIRY TALES AND CASTLES

If you are into fairy tales, motor down the 370-mile (600-km) Fairy-Tale Road where the attractions revolve around the stories contrived by Wilhelm and Jacob Grimm—of Grimm Fairy Tale fame. In Alsfeld, located in central Germany, visitors can visit the House of Little Red Riding Hood. Farther down the highway is also Sababurg Castle, most commonly known as the Sleeping Beauty Castle.

# TEXT-DEPENDENT QUESTIONS

1. In which part of Germany is the city of Leipzig located?
2. Explain the importance of the Rhine River.
3. Where does the Rhine River begin, and where does it end?

# RESEARCH PROJECTS

1. Research German fairy tales and see if you can pinpoint the location of some of these stories on a map. Place pushpins to mark the locations. Write down the name of the fairy tale on a slip of paper and tack it to the map.
2. Use the library and Internet to research one of Germany's famous castles and write a short history about it.

Historic Heidelberg, Germany's oldest university town.

# FURTHER RESEARCH

**Online**

Visit the Central Intelligence Agency's World Factbook on Germany for statistics, a brief history, and maps: https://www.cia.gov/library/publications/the-world-factbook/geos/gm.html.

Learn more about tourism in Germany by visiting http://www.germany.travel/en/index.html.

Learn more about German food and where you can find a German restaurant near you by visiting http://www.germanfoodguide.com.

**Books**

Fulbrook, Mary. *A Concise History of Germany*. Cambridge: Cambridge University Press, 2004.

Knuth, Christopher. *The German Kitchen: Traditional Recipes, Regional Favorites*. Northampton, MA: Interlink Pub Group, 2013.

Watson, Peter. *The German Genius: Europe's Third Renaissance, the Second Scientific Revolution, and the Twentieth Century*. New York: Harper Perennial, 2011.

NOTE TO EDUCATORS: This book contains both imperial and metric measurements as well as references to global practices and trends in an effort to encourage the student to gain a worldly perspective. We, as publishers, feel it's our role to give young adults the tools they need to thrive in a global society.

# SERIES GLOSSARY

**ancestral**: relating to ancestors, or relatives who have lived in the past.

**archaeologist**: a scientist that investigates past societies by digging in the earth to examine their remains.

**artisanal**: describing something produced on a small scale, usually handmade by skilled craftspeople.

**colony**: a settlement in another country or place that is controlled by a "home" country.

**commonwealth**: an association of sovereign nations unified by common cultural, political, and economic interests and traits.

**communism**: a social and economic philosophy characterized by a classless society and the absence of private property.

**continent**: any of the seven large land masses that constitute most of the dry land on the surface of the earth.

**cosmopolitan**: worldly; showing the influence of many cultures.

**culinary**: relating to the kitchen, cookery, and style of eating.

**cultivated**: planted and harvested for food, as opposed to the growth of plants in the wild.

**currency**: a system of money.

**demographics**: the study of population trends.

**denomination**: a religious grouping within a faith that has its own organization.

**dynasty**: a ruling family that extends across generations, usually in an autocratic form of government, such as a monarchy.

**ecosystems**: environments where interdependent organisms live.

**endemic**: native, or not introduced, to a particular region, and not naturally found in other areas.

**exile**: absence from one's country or home, usually enforced by a government for political or religious reasons.

**feudal**: a system of economic, political, or social organization in which poor landholders are subservient to wealthy landlords; used mostly in relation to the Middle Ages.

**globalization**: the processes relating to increasing international exchange that have resulted in faster, easier connections across the world.

**gross national product**: the measure of all the products and services a country produces in a year.

**heritage**: tradition and history.

**homogenization**: the process of blending elements together, sometimes resulting in a less interesting mixture.

**iconic**: relating to something that has become an emblem or symbol.

**idiom**: the language particular to a community or class; usually refers to regular, "everyday" speech.

**immigrants**: people who move to and settle in a new country.

**indigenous**: originating in and naturally from a particular region or country.

**industrialization**: the process by which a country changes from a farming society to one that is based on industry and manufacturing.

# SERIES GLOSSARY

**integration**: the process of opening up a place, community, or organization to all types of people.

**kinship**: web of social relationships that have a common origin derived from ancestors and family.

**literacy rate**: the percentage of people who can read and write.

**matriarchal**: of or relating to female leadership within a particular group or system.

**migrant**: a person who moves from one place to another, usually for reasons of employment or economic improvement.

**militarized**: warlike or military in character and thought.

**missionary**: one who goes on a journey to spread a religion.

**monopoly**: a situation where one company or state controls the market for an industry or product.

**natural resources**: naturally occurring materials, such as oil, coal, and gold, that can be used by people.

**nomadic**: describing a way of life in which people move, usually seasonally, from place to place in search of food, water, and pastureland.

**nomadic**: relating to people who have no fixed residence and move from place to place.

**parliament**: a body of government responsible for enacting laws.

**patriarchal**: of or relating to male leadership within a particular group or system.

**patrilineal**: relating to the relationship based on the father or the descendants through the male line.

**polygamy**: the practice of having more than one spouse.

**provincial**: belonging to a province or region outside of the main cities of a country.

**racism**: prejudice or animosity against people belonging to other races.

**ritualize**: to mark or perform with specific behaviors or observances.

**sector**: part or aspect of something, especially of a country's or region's economy.

**secular**: relating to worldly concerns; not religious.

**societal**: relating to the order, structure, or functioning of society or community.

**socioeconomic**: relating to social and economic factors, such as education and income, often used when discussing how classes, or levels of society, are formed.

**statecraft**: the ideas about and methods of running a government.

**traditional**: relating to something that is based on old historical ways of doing things.

**urban sprawl**: the uncontrolled expansion of urban areas away from the center of the city into remote, outlying areas.

**urbanization**: the increasing movement of people from rural areas to cities, usually in search of economic improvement, and the conditions resulting this migration.

# INDEX

*Italicized page numbers* refer to illustrations.

**A**

Advent traditions 21
Airbus 37
aircraft industry 37
Alps 50–51
Appleyard, Brian 46
architecture *18, 40, 48,* 53, *53*
Arminius 9
art and design 45–47, *46*
Austria 12, 26–27, 44–45, 50–51
autobahn 52–53
automobile industry 36–37, 39, *39*
Aygun, Mahmut 26

**B**

Bach, Johann Sebastian 43, *43*
Bachfest (Leipzig) 43, *43*
Bauhaus building *40*
Bavaria 26, 29–30, 44–45, *45,* 49, 49–50, *54*
Bayreuth Opera Festival 44
Beatles, The 44, *44,* 47
Becker, Boris 43
beer *23,* 28–31, *29,* 31, 32
Beethoven, Ludwig van 43
Benz, Karl Friedrich 36
Berchtesgaden *18*
Berlin *35,* 41, 42, *42,* 53, *53*
Berlin Wall 14, *14,* 41, 53
birth rate 19
Bismarck, Otto von *12,* 12–13, 15
Black Forest 51, *51*
BMW automobiles 36, *36*
Bonfire band *47*
Brahms, Johannes 43
Brandenburg Gate *8*
bratwurst *26,* 27
bread 28–29, *29*
Bremen 28

**C**

Caesar, Julius Gaius 9
Canada 30
capitalism 15
castles 49, 51, 54, *54,* 54–55
Catholic Church 10–12, 15
Charlemagne 10, *10*
children 19–20, *34,* 34–35
Christianity 9–12
Christmas 20, *20–21, 21,* 22, 50
cities 52–54, *53*
classical music 43
coal 13, 37–39
communism 12–13, 15
concentration camps 13
contemporary music 44
culinary traditions 25–26, 31
cultural heritage 11, 20, 44, 46, 50, 52

**D**

Daimler, Gottlieb 36
dancing 45, *45*
Danube River 50
"Day in the Life: What Makes the Average
        German Tick?" (Spiegel) 23
demographics 19, 23
Diet of Worms 11
*döner kebap* 26
Dresden *15*
Duisburg *38*
dumplings 27

**E**

Easter 22, *22*
Eastern Europe 14, *14,* 38
East Germany 14, 15, 19, 36
economy *13,* 13–14, 17, 26, 33, 36–38, 39
education 33–36, *34*

# INDEX

Einstein, Albert 33, 34
employment 13, 19, 36, 38
energy resources 36
European Union 26, 36

**F**
fairy tales 54–55
family roles and traditions *19*, 19–20, 23
Feuerbach, Anselm *46*
Final Solution 13
Fish Market *28*
folk music (*volksmusick*) 44–45
food and culinary traditions *25*, 25–31
Forbach River *51*
France 10, 13–14, 43
Franconia 49–50
Frankfurt *20*, 27, 37
frankfurter 27
Franks *10*
friendship 22
Fuerstenzug mural (Dresden) *15*

**G**
geography 49–53
Georghehner, Johann 27
German, Sam 30
German chocolate cake 30
Germanic tribes 9–10
German states' unification 12
*gesamtschule* 35
globalization of economy 37
Graf, Steffi 43
Great Britain 13–14, 45
Great Depression 13
Greece 25
Grimm, Wilhelm and Jacob 54
Gropius, Walter *40*
*grundschule* (basic school) 35
guest workers program 19, 53

gymnasium (high school) 35
gypsies 13

**H**
Hamburg 37, *37*, 44
Handel, George Frederick 43
Hapsburg Empire 12
Heidelberg 54, *55*
Henry I (king of Germany) 52
Hertz, Gustav 33
high school (gymnasium) 35
Hindemith, Paul 43
history 9–15
Hitler, Adolf 13, *13*
holiday celebrations and traditions *16*, 20, 20–22. *See also* Christmas
Holy Roman Empire 9–10
homosexuals 13
hot dog 27
Huber, Anke 43
Humboldt University (Berlin) *35*

**I**
immigrants 18–19, 25, 26, 31, 38, 53
indulgences (Catholic Church) 10–11
industrial production 36–38, *38*
intermediate school (*realschule*) 35
*Iphigenie* (Feuerbach) *46*
Iraq 18

**J**
Japan 39
Jews 13
Julius Caesar 9
Jung von Matt company 17–18

# INDEX

**K**

kale 28, *28*
Kiefer, Anselm 45–46

**L**

Lake Constance 50, *50*
*länd* (state) 34–35
Ländler dance 45
landscape 49–53
Leipzig *43*, 54, 55
Lennon, John *44*
literacy rate 33
Ludwig I (crown prince of Bavaria) 30
Luther, Martin 10–12, *11*, 15, 20
Lutheranism 11–12

**M**

marriage 19. *See also* family roles and
        traditions
Marx, Karl 12
mentally disabled 13
Mercedes-Benz 36, *39*
miracle plays 20
Moser, Joseph 27
Müller, Thomas and Sabine 17–18
Munich 30, 36, 38
music 42–45, *43*, 47, *47*, 53

**N**

national character 17–18
Nazi Party 13
Netherlands 51
Neuschwanstein castle *54*
ninety-five theses 11

**O**

Oktoberfest 29–30, *30*, 42
Otto the Great (Holy Roman emperor) 10

**P**

Planck, Max 33, 54
*polterabend* 22
pope, role of 11–12
Porsche 36
potatoes *24*, 25, *26*, 27, 28
power politics 12
pretzels *31*
Protestant Reformation 11–12, 15
Prussia 12

**Q**

Quadriga statue (Berlin) *8*
Quedlinburg 52, *52*

**R**

railroad 37, *37*
realpolitik 12–13, 15
*realschule* (intermediate school) 35
Reinheitsgebot law 29, 31
religion 9–12, 15
Rhine River 50–51, 55
Richter, Gerhard 46
Romans 9
Ruhr region *38*

**S**

sauerkraut 25, *27*, 28
sausage *26*, 26–28, 31
schnapps 28
schnitzel *24*
Schuhplattler dance *45*
Schumacher, Michael 43
Schumann, Robert 43
Schütz, Heinrich 43
seafood 28
secondary schools 35
Sleeping Beauty castle 54
soccer 41–42, *42*, 47

# INDEX

social-market economy 37
South Korea 39
Soviet Union 13–14
sports 41–43, *50*
steel industry *38*
Stich, Michael 43
Switzerland 50–51
Syria 18

**T**
television 46, 47
tennis 43
Therese (crown princess of Bavaria) 30
trade 26, *37*
traditional music and arts 44–45, *45*
transportation system 37, 52–53
Treaty of Versailles (1919) *13*,13
Turkish immigrants 18–19, 25–26, 38, 53

**U**
unemployment 13
unification after Cold War 14, 36
United States 13–14, 22, 23, 30
universities 35–36, 39
University of Heidelberg 54

**V**
vocational education 35
Volkswagen 36

**W**
Wagner, Richard 43–44
war reparations 13
wedding traditions *21*, 21–22, 23
*weisswurst* 27
West Germany 14, 15, 19
"Wetten Dass...?" 46–47
wiener 27
women's roles 19
workforce 13, 19, 36, 38
World Cup 41–42, *42*, 47
World War I 13, *13*
World War II 13–14, 39

**Z**
zones of occupation 13–14

# PHOTO CREDITS

| Page | Page Location | Archive/Photographer |
|------|---------------|----------------------|
| 6 | Full page | Dreamstime/Leonid Andronov |
| 8 | Top | Dreamstime/Aladin66 |
| 10 | Top left | Dreamstime/Jorisvo |
| 11 | Bottom left | Dollar Photo Club/nmann77 |
| 12 | Top left | Wikimedia Commons |
| 13 | Bottom left | Wikimedia Commons/William Orpen |
| 14 | Middle | Dreamstime/Markwaters |
| 14 | Bottom | Dreamstime/Noppasinw |
| 15 | Bottom | Dreamstime/Sergiy Palamarchuk |
| 16 | Top | Dreamstime/Dieter Hawlan |
| 18 | Bottom | Dreamstime/Daniel M. Cisillino |
| 19 | Top right | Dollar Photo Club/famveldman |
| 20 | Top | Dreamstime/Horst Lieber |
| 21 | Bottom | Wikimedia Commons/Silar |
| 22 | Bottom left | iStock.com/hsvrs |
| 23 | Bottom | Dreamstime/Robert Kneschke |
| 24 | Top | Dreamstime/Peteer |
| 26 | Bottom left | Dreamstime/Osvaldodip |
| 27 | Top left | Dreamstime/Kabvisio |
| 28 | Bottom left | Dreamstime/Darius Dzinnik |
| 28 | Bottom right | Dreamstime/Frank Gärtner |
| 29 | Top | Dreamstime/Gunold Brunbauer |
| 29 | Bottom right | Dreamstime/Venemama |
| 30 | Top | Dreamstime/Pavel Losevsky |
| 31 | Bottom | Dreamstime/Elena Schweitzer |

| Page | Page Location | Archive/Photographer |
|------|---------------|----------------------|
| 32 | Top | Dreamstime/Arne9001 |
| 34 | Top | Dreamstime/Dieniti |
| 35 | Bottom | Dreamstime/Buschmen |
| 36 | Bottom right | Dreamstime/Jdanne |
| 37 | Top left | Dreamstime/T.w. Van Urk |
| 37 | Top right | Dreamstime/Alptraum |
| 38 | Bottom | Dreamstime/Stephan Pietzko |
| 39 | Bottom | Dreamstime/Typhoonski |
| 40 | Top | Dreamstime/Camille Tsang |
| 42 | Bottom | Dreamstime/Markwaters |
| 43 | Top | Dreamstime/Claudiodivizia |
| 44 | Bottom left | Dreamstime/Gors4730 |
| 45 | Top | iStock.com/filmfoto |
| 46 | Top left | Wikimedia Commons/Anslem Feuerbach |
| 47 | Bottom | Dreamstime/Dimitar Marinov |
| 48 | Top | Dreamstime/Ton Vermeesch |
| 50 | Top | Dreamstime/Gunold Brunbauer |
| 51 | Bottom | Dreamstime/Edith Czech |
| 52 | Top | Dreamstime/T.w. Van Urk |
| 53 | Bottom | Dreamstime/Rudi1976 |
| 54 | Top | Dreamstime/Matyas Rehak |
| 55 | Bottom | Dreamstime/Sage78 |

## COVER

| Top | Dreamstime/Matthew Dixon |
|-----|--------------------------|
| Bottom left | Dollar Photo Club/Antonio Gravante |
| Bottom right | Dollar Photo Club/BeTa-Artworks |

# ABOUT THE AUTHOR

**John Perritano** is an award-winning journalist, writer, and editor from Southbury, Connecticut, who has written numerous articles and books on history, culture, and science for publishers that include National Geographic's *Reading Expedition Series* and its *Global Issues Series*, focusing on such topics as globalization, population, and natural resources. He has also been a contributor to Discovery.com, *Popular Mechanics*, and other magazines and websites. He holds a master's degree in American History from Western Connecticut State University.